Apostolic Succession.

"This wisdom descendeth not from above, but is earthly, sensual, devilish."—James, cap. 3, verse 15.

BY

ANGLO-SAXON.

LONDON:

ELLIOT STOCK, 61, PATERNOSTER ROW, E.C.,

1876.

APOSTOLIC SUCCESSION.

APOSTOLIC SUCCESSION.

"The Church of England desires to include within her pale
both those who hold the doctrine of the Apostolic Succession, and those who do not. To meet the need of the
latter she nowhere requires any of her members or
ministers to hold the doctrine. To meet the need of the
former she provides that all her ministers should profess
that succession as a fact."

*Reply of F. Exon (Bishop Temple) to Count Poveleri—
di Vicenza.*

The above has been published as the reply of an Eng-
lish Protestant Bishop to a Protestant foreigner, who had
written to ask the Bishop if "Apostolic Succession" was
a doctrine of the Church of England. The reply is a singular
one. Up to the time of reading it I had not examined the
subject of Apostolic Succession with anything like the
serious attention it demands, but when I read the Bishop's
reply two questions presented themselves to my mind.
1. Do the Holy Scriptures of the New Testament—the
written canon and authority for the Christian faith—give
any warrant for such a doctrine? 2. Is it one of the
articles of belief authorised and promulgated in any legal
written form by the Protestant Episcopal Church of Eng-

land, and required by it (as **Dr. Temple** says) to be professed by its ministers ? To satisfy **my mind** upon the first and chief question, I carefully examined the New Testament for the history of the appointment of the Apostles, and other orders in the Primitive Christian Church, as made by our Lord in His lifetime, or by His representatives, the twelve Apostles, who had after His death, resurrection, and ascension, with a full knowledge of His views, the responsibility of completing the organization of His visible Church. In Matthew, c. 4, v. 18 to 21—the account is given of our Lord calling Simon Peter, Andrew, James, and John; and in c. 9, **v. 9,** the call of Matthew to become His disciple. In c. 10, v. 2 to 4, these five, with seven others, are recorded as having been appointed to be Apostles ; and as the circumstances of this appointment are of vital consequence in discussing the question, I will give them a little in detail. " These twelve Jesus sent forth " :—Simon Peter, Andrew, James, John, Philip, Bartholomew, Thomas, Matthias, James, Thaddeus, Simon, Judas ; and they received the following instructions : They were not to go into the way of the Gentiles, nor enter any city of the Samaritans, but to go only to the Children of the House of Israel. 2. They were to preach " the kingdom of Heaven is at hand." 3. They were to provide neither gold, silver or brass, nor scrip, nor two coats, neither shoes nor staves. 4. And as they had freely received, so they had freely to give; and they received (at this time) power to do the following—1. Heal the sick. 2. Cleanse the lepers. 3. Raise the dead. 4. Cast out devils.

The closing remark of our Lord, "for the workman is worthy of his hire"—coming as it does on the injunction not to acquire money for the expenses of their journey, but accept the voluntary support which would be provided for them—was in few words telling them not to make a trade of their gifts, and also shewing how professing Christians in all time to come should provide for the faithful labourer. The twelve Apostles are elsewhere called disciples, and included with the rest of the infant Church; but it is evident that they alone were specially appointed for the purpose I shall hereafter call attention to; and though our Lord had other followers and believers in His mission, the number of whom is given as above one-hundred-and-twenty, it is to be marked that none but the Apostles were, by special appointment of our Lord, to meet Him after His resurrection—Matthew, 28 c., v. 16. " Then the eleven disciples went away into Galilee into a mountain where Jesus had appointed them, and when they saw him they worshipped, but some doubted." So far Matthew's record. Mark gives the same account of the call of the first five disciples, and a similar statement to that of Matthew, of the appointment of the Apostles—Mark, c. l, v. 16 to 20; c. 3, v. 13 to 19—and in c. 6, v. 7 to 12, their instructions, with but little variation from these recorded by Matthew, but with the addition that they had to go forth " two by two " without however assigning the reason. At v. 30, is the account of the Apostles returning to Jesus, giving Him an account of what they had done and taught. Before proceeding

with the various narratives of the Evangelists, it
may be well to remark that not only was it
the Apostles alone that had the appointment to
meet our Lord after His resurrection, but it was
from the Apostles alone that our Lord took witnesses to
His transfiguration, and to hear these words from heaven—
"This is my beloved Son, hear him;" and that when the
Passover was to be celebrated, and the Lord's Supper
instituted, the twelve Apostles only sat down to
meat with Him, thus establishing, I think con-
clusively, that the Apostles were a separate order
of Church officers appointed for a special purpose
to be hereafter developed. That they felt their
rising pre-eminence is evident from the breaking out
of sacerdotal pride on the part of two of their number
(John and James), which is recorded in Matthew, 20 c,
and v. 20, which our Lord rebuked in the following
words: " Ye know that they which are accounted to rule
over the Gentiles exercise lordship over them, and their
great ones exercise authority upon them, but it shall not
be so among you, but whosoever will be great among you
shall be servant of all." In passing I would submit the above
to the calm reflection of professing ministers of the Gospel
of our Lord and Saviour Jesus Christ, who assume the
titles of " His Holiness," " His Eminence," " Right Rev.
Father in God," "Lord Bishop," &c., &c. To continue the
Gospel narratives, Mark, c. 16, v. 14, gives the same
statement as Matthew of the appearance to, and conversa-
tion after His resurrection, with the eleven in Galilee

where, at meat He upbraided them for the hardness of their hearts. Luke gives, in c. 6, v. 12, his account of the Apostles, with the additional information that, before their appointment, our Saviour went into a mountain to pray, and continued all night " in prayer to God;" and when it was day called unto Him His disciples, from whom He chose twelve whom He named " Apostles." He also gives the class of powers they were invested with, and the directions for their guidance, and records their return to Jesus to report what they had done. He next gives, in c. 10, v. 1 to 16, the appointment of seventy other disciples to proclaim the advent of the Gospel. " After these things the Lord appointed other seventy also, and sent them ' two and two' before His face into every city and place whither he himself would come." The instructions and powers given them seem to have been nearly the same as those given the Apostles; so that the mere possession of miraculous powers alone could not have constituted the Apostolic qualification. The seventy also returned to our Lord to report the results of their mission, which it is said they did " with joy." Luke next records another outbreak of pride among the Apostles, c. 22, v. 24; and our Lord's rebuke, conveyed in similar terms to those He used on the first occasion quoted. Luke closes with the appearance of our Lord to the eleven. Next is John's Gospel, which is silent as to the appointment of the Apostles, but gives the same statement as that made in the other Gospels of our Lord's appearance to His Apostles after His death and resurrection, with the statement that Thomas was the chief unbeliever in the reality of the resurrection of our Saviour. To him our Lord shewed such proofs as convinced that Apostle that he did indeed see his Master who had suffered and died on the Cross.

I have now gone over the record of the Gospels as to the call and appointment of the Apostles, their directions, and powers. One other power than these I have named is stated by the advocates and defenders of Apostolic Succession to have been conferred, first upon Peter, then on all the Apostles—viz., the personal "power of forgiving sins;" and the anxiety to have the name of possessing the power of useing this in the sense and manner of the Church of Rome, no doubt is the origin of the bold assumption and obstinate defence of the so-called doctrine of " Apostolic Succession "—both by Romanists and their auxiliaries in the Church of England. The portion of Scripture in which this power is professed to be found is Matthew c. 16, v. 13 to 19, and is as follows: " He saith unto them, But whom say ye that I am? and Simon Peter answered and said, Thou art the Christ the Son of the living God. And Jesus answered and said unto him, Blessed art thou Simon Barjonas, for flesh and blood hath not revealed it unto thee, but my Father which is in Heaven; and I say also unto thee that thou art Peter, and upon this rock I wll build my Church, and the gates of Hell shalt not prevail against it, and I will give unto thee the keys of the Kingdom of Heaven, and whatsoever thou shall bind on earth shall be bound in Heaven, and whatsoever thou shalt loose on earth shalt be loosed in Heaven." Now

Peter not only never seems to have felt that he was the rock upon which the Church would be built, but for the benefit of the Church, when living, plainly taught that the rock was Christ, the head corner-stone; See Acts, c. 4, v. 11. When the high priests and others questioned Peter, "By what power or by what name" he had cured the lame man at the temple gate called Beautiful, he replied, "Being filled with the Holy Ghost:" " Be it known unto you all and to all the people of Israel, that by the name of Jesus Christ, of Nazareth, whom ye crucified, whom God raised from the dead, even by him doth this man stand before you whole. This is the stone which was set at naught of you builders, which has become the head of the corner, neither is there salvation by any other." And he is as clear in his Epistle 1st, c. 2, v. 3 to 8:—" If so be ye have tasted the Lord is gracious, to whom coming as unto a living stone, disallowed—indeed of men but chosen of God and precious. Ye also as living stones are built up a spiritual house " . . . . Wherefore also it is contained in the Scripture, " Behold I lay in Sion a chief corner stone, and he that believeth on him shall not be confounded, but unto them which be disobedient the stone which the builders disallowed the same is made the head of the corner, and a stone of stumbling and a rock of offence." So much for Peter being the rock on which the Church is built. It is evident he never thought so, and the utterances of the Church of Rome on the subject may be disposed of in Peter's own words, that they are "cunningly devised fables." The second instance adduced of the power to forgive sins being bestowed upon the Apostles, is in John c. 20 v. 22 to 23, where at the appearance of our Lord after his resurrection to his Apostles, it is stated He "Breathed upon them" and said, "Receive the Holy Ghost whosoever sins ye remit they are remitted, and whosesoever sins ye retain they are retained." Whatever this power was, that it was not a personal power is plain, and the Apostles never understood it to be so, and taught quite a different doctrine from that sought to be enforced by the Church of Rome and others. It is alone, however, of so much consequence to be correctly described, that it will be made the subject of another letter. But before proceeding with the question of "Apostolic Succession" I must call upon the defenders of Apostolic Succession to show why, of all the Apostolic gifts, they now only claim the "power of forgiving sins" —if ever such a power was bestowed upon the Apostles— which I deny. And I ask why, if they are successors of the Apostles, they do not continue to exercise the other Apostolic powers, of "healing the sick, cleansing the lepers, raising the dead," and above all do not use what would be invaluable in missionary labour—"the gift of tongues?" Awaiting their reply, I proceed with the history of the Christian Church, and will endeavour to place before my readers what constituted the qualification of an Apostle, and to show the impossibility of that qualification being found after the first generation of disciples. Our Lord had now returned to heaven, and the Church was to commence the great work for which it was created. The Apostles with the other disciples made Jerusalem their place of assembly, and the first act of Church Government was the appointment of one of the disciples to fill the office of Apostle, vacant by the fall of Judas: and so important is its bearing on the question of Apostolic Succession that I must give it as full as possible. It is contained in Acts cap. I. v. 15. "And in those days Peter stood up in the midst of the disciples" (the number of which together was about one hundred and twenty), and after detailing the crime of Judas, and how he fell, makes this remarkable exposition of the qualification requisite for an Apostle, v. 23—"*Wherefore of these men who have companied with us all the time that the Lord Jesus went in and out among us, beginning from the baptism of John, and unto the same day he was taken up from us, must one be ordained to be a witness of his resurrection.*" Now here, I do not hesitate to say, is to be found the all essential mark of an Apostle—"a witness with us of his resurrection," hence the special privileges given the Apostles throughout our Lord's Ministry in contradistinction to those accorded to the seventy, whose office and ministrations were confined to going before Him as heralds to such places as He would visit. That this is the Apostolic qualification, I think is fully confirmed by the testimony of the Apostles in Acts, c. 2, v. 32, "This Jesus hath God raised up, whereof we are all witnesses;" c. 4, v. 23, "And with great power give the Apostles witness of the resurrection of the Lord Jesus;" c. 5, v. 31, "Him hath God exalted to his right hand to be a Prince and a Saviour . . . "

v. 32, "And we are his witnesses of these things;" c. 1,
v. 39, "And we are witnesses of all things which he did;"
v. 40, "Him God raised up the third day and shewed him
openly, not to all the people, but unto *witnesses chosen
before of God, even to us, who did eat and drink with
him after he rose from the dead;*" c. 13, vs. 30-31,
"But God raised him from the dead, and he was
seen many days of them which came up with him
from Galilee to Jerusalem, who are his witnesses unto the
people." And Peter, in his Epistle, 2nd, 1 c. vs. 16, 17, 18,
says, "for we have not followed cunningly devised fables
when we made known unto you the power and coming of
our Lord Jesus Christ, but were eye-witnesses of his
majesty, for he received from God the Father honor and
glory, when there came such a voice to him from the
excellent glory ' This is my beloved son, in whom I am
well pleased,' and this voice which came from heaven we
heard when we were with him on the Holy Mount."

The mode of proceeding to appoint the successor to
Judas was so simple and so different to the modern method
of appointing a Bishop by *conge d'elire*, that a full detail of
it is desirable here, Acts, c. 1 v. 23, 6, "And they appointed two: Joseph, called Barnabas, who was surnamed
Justus, and Matthias; and they prayed and said, Thou
Lord, which knowest the hearts of all men, shew whether
of these two thou hast chosen, that he may take part of this
Ministry and Apostleship from which Judas by transgres-
sion fell, that he might go to his own place, and they gave
forth their lot, and the lot fell upon Matthias, and he was

numbered with the eleven Apostles." So ended, in this plain, pious form, grand in its very simplicity, the first act of government of the Christian Church. It will be observed the Apostles of their own power did not appoint the successor of Judas, but that they called together the Disciples to nominate two persons having the qualification, and the Lord was then, by prayer, asked to select the individual to fill the vacant office. The next record gives the appointment of deacons to relieve the Apostles of the labour of distributing the charity of the Church, or, as it is termed, "to serve tables." Here again the Twelve called the Disciples together, and requested them to select seven men, which, when they had done, these seven were, after prayer, set apart for this purpose. There now arose a new feature in the Church. My readers will remember the first Twelve Apostles were not to go to any but the children of Israel. Now, the Gentiles were to have the Gospel offered them, and preparatory to this Paul was called to the Apostleship by a special revelation, which is given in Acts 26, v. 15 to 18, " And I said, who art thou Lord? And he said, I am he whom thou persecutest—but rise, stand upon thy feet, for I have appeared unto thee for this purpose to make thee a minister and a witness both of these things in the which I will appear unto thee, delivering thee from the people, and from the Gentiles, unto whom I now send thee, to open their eyes and turn them from darkness to light, from the power of Satan to God ;" and in c 22, v. 12. it is stated, Annanias, a devout man, came to him (Paul) and said, " The God of our Fathers hath chosen

thee that thou shouldest know his will, and see that Just
One, and shouldest hear the voice of his mouth, for thou
shall be a witness unto all men of what thou hast seen and
heard." And Paul further states that "while I prayed in
the Temple I was in a trance, and saw Him saying unto
me, Make haste and get thee quickly out of Jerusalem,
30 v. 21, for I will send thee far hence unto the Gentiles."
If any strong confirmation was required to show what was
the qualification of an Apostle, and the purpose for which
the office was created, it is surely given in the appearance
of the Lord to Paul, to make him a witness, and give him the
requisite status to become what the Lord design ed him to be
—an Apostle to the Gentiles. That Joses, who will shortly
appear in the narrative, had the requisite qualification
cannot be doubted, as he seems to have been an old
disciple, well known to the Apostles, by whom, for his good
qualities, he had been surnamed Barnabas, the son of con-
solation, and who had sold his land, and laid it at the
the Apostle's feet; and who is further described as "a good
man, and full of the Holy Ghost and faith;" the time now
approached when the Jews, having in Paul's words,
' judged themselves unworthy of everlasting life,' the
Gentiles were to have the Gospel preached unto them, and
this our Lord decided should be done by two disciples,
specially appointed Apostles to labour with the Gentiles,
and the Holy Ghost directed the Church at Antioch to
separate Paul and Barnabas for the work whereunto he
had called them, which, having fasted and prayed, they
did, and the record ends. "So they, being sent forth by

the Holy Ghost, departed." Paul and Barnabas acted together but a short time, and hereafter Paul only is conspicuous in the Gospel narrative. This is the last record of the appointment of any other disciple to the office of an Apostle. And there will not be found any trace of a promise to continue the office with powers, or directions to fill vacancies, or any attempt by the Apostles or disciples so to do. No. the Apostolic office closed with the last appointment of Paul and Barnabas. The twelve Apostles were appointed to preach to the Jews only, but the two last (Paul and Barnabas) were appointed to preach to the Gentiles—to be witnesses, each in their assigned field of labour, of Christ's resurrection. That these appointments were not made without considerable opposition and dissatisfaction on the part of the Jewish proselytes and others, is quite evident. Peter had his share of contending for its validity; and Paul, to the close of his career, continually reiterates that he was an Apostle, and fully possessed the qualifications of an Apostle—viz., having seen the Lord Jesus after his resurrection, and was so enabled to be one of his witnesses; this will be seen by reference to his Epistles—Romans, 1st c. 4th v. Paul, a servant of Jesus Christ, called to be an Apostle; 1st Corinthians, 1st c., 1st v., Paul, called to be an Apostle of Jesus Christ through the will of God, in c. 15, 15th v., he declares that he had preached that Christ had risen again the third day, and had been seen of the disciples; and, "last of all, was seen of me also as one born out of due time," "for I am the least of the Apostles;" and, again, in 2nd

Corinthians, 1st c., 1st v. Paul, an Apostle of Jesus Christ, by the will of God; and in 2nd Corinthians, 12th c., 11th v., Paul asserts that in nothing is he behind the chiefest Apostles. In Galatians, 1st c., 1st verse, "Paul, an Apostle, not of men, neither by man, but by Jesus Christ, and God the Father who raised him from the dead," and so on through his Epistles he is always combatting in some form the opponents of his claim to the Apostleship, shewing clearly, I think, that there was a special qualification required for the office, and the strong feeling on the part of the Church that this qualification could only be found in those whom Peter's words had "companied with us all the time the Lord Jesus went in and out among us, beginning with the baptism of John unto the same day that he was taken up from us." "Must one be ordained to be a witness with us of his resurrection." It is evident, therefore, that if Peter's description of the qualification required for an Apostle was correct—and who can doubt it?—the qualification could not be found after the death of the first generation of disciples, and thus, of necessity, the office of an Apostle would cease. There is no evidence or example of any other ordinations of Apostles, except that of Matthias at Jerusalem, and of Paul and Barnabas at Autioch. Neither are there any instructions direct, or indirect, or inferential, for the continuance of the office. The first twelve Apostles were appointed for the Jews, and the two last for the Gentiles Thus, the two great sections of the world being provided for, the office ceased, as did the gift of tongues, which, after all the then known world, had some who in their own tongue could communicate the wonderful things God had revealed, and "that the Kingdom of Heaven was at hand" alike with the Apostolic office—ceased. It has always seemed remarkable to me that the upholders of Apostolic Succession, and claiming to be such successors, should have ceased to use all or any of their predecessors' power, except what the Apostles never claimed to possess—the personal "power of forgiving sins." I now close the consideration of the first question—"Do the Scriptures of the New Testament, the written canon and authority for the Christian faith, give any warrant for such a doctrine—viz., "Apostolical Succession?" and I trust I have produced as strong a conviction in the minds of my readers as there is in my own—that there is no warrant in Scripture for any such doctrine. And I wish the advocates of "Apostolic Succession" would show, if they are successors of the Apostles, why they do not exercise all the powers the Apostles had? And to state when, where, and by what authority, the successors of the Apostles (if they had any), had the choice give them to cease from using their powers to heal the sick, and raise the dead, and to only use the power of personally forgiving sins, which they say the Apostles had. I now proceed to my second question, "Is it one of the articles of belief, authorised and promulgated in any legal form by the Protestant Episcopal Church of England, and required by it, as Dr. Temple says, to be professed by its ministry?" I cannot find it in the Constitution, and Canons the 39 Articles, Homilies or

Catechism—and unless it lurks in the Ordination Service of Archbishops, Bishops, and Priests,—it is not to be found in any shape which can be regarded as a legal enactment binding on its ministers or members, it may be meant in the words ordered to be addressed by the Archbishop the Bishop undergoing the rite of ordination, viz., " Receive the Holy Ghost," "by the imposition of our hands," this however may be a mere form and have as little meaning, as the requests made by the Archbishop. 1st, that the Queen's Mandate be read ; 2nd, that they " fall to prayer," "before we admit and send forth this person presented to us" part of the prayer being " that it may please Thee to bless this our Brother *elected*." These gentlemen knowing quite well that the " Brother " is not elected or nominated by the Church as Matthias was, or indeed " elected " at all by anybody in the ordinary meaning of that word, but is fixed upon and sent by the Sovereign or Prime Minister of the day to be ordained a Bishop, and that no collective body or set of persons in the Church of England, has any power of either freely electing or rejecting him, but that once fixed upon by the Crown, he is sure to be made a Bishop—the doctrine of " Apostolic succession," may as described by Dr. Temple be taught in all this extraordinary proceeding,—but of Apostolic practice there is none,—are we therefore driven to believe there is really nothing in it but that this service is drawn up to run all fours to coun- tenance the singular ceremony to create a very singular office, viz., that of a " priest,"—singular in any Christian Church,—but more so in a Protestant Church. In the early Christian Church, there were Apostles, Prophets Evangelists, Pastors, Overseers, Elders, Ministers, Teachers and Deacons appointed "for the perfecting of the Saints for the work of the Ministry, for the edifying of the Body of Christ.—" but "a priest," is not to be found named in any of the officers appointed by our Lord, during his sojourn on earth, or after His ascension, by any revelation made by the Holy Ghost to the Church, and Paul in his Epistle to the Hebrews fully sets forth the reasons why a "priest" was not required, and could not exist in the Christian Dispensation, for our Saviour was our High Priest, "who needeth not daily as those High Priests" (Paul is speaking of the Jewish,) "to offer up sacrifice first for his own sins and then for the people's; for this he did *once*, when he offered himself," and affirms that, "this man after he had offered *one* sacrifice for sins *for ever*, sat down at the right hand of God"—and further affirms to close his argument that the "Lord saith I will put my laws into their hearts and in their minds, I will write them ; and their sins and iniquities will I remember no more. Now where remission of these is, there is *no more offering for sin*," however the Church of England has got such an officer, but debars him by the 31st Article from offering sacrifices for sin ; however this does not stop the creation of "priests" by the Bishop, who when making them uses the following words. "Receive the Holy Ghost for the work and office of a priest," "by the imposition of our hands," "whose sins thou dost forgive, they are forgiven and whose sins thou dost retain they are retained." This is I presume the outcrop of the "Apostolic Succession," dimly outlined by by Dr. Temple in his reply to Count Provoleri, if so it is a pity the ordaining Bishop does not confer all the Apostolic powers (in the order they were bestowed upon the Apostles,) upon the candidates for the priesthood who he is supposed to be making successors to the Apostles. Not doing so leaves them in a very sorry plight—left by the 31st Article to be "priests" in name only—this deficiency in the ordination service makes them only the fractional part of an Apostle. However as all the goodmen of the Church of England from the time of the Reformation have firmly opposed popery and re-pudiated (some at the cost of their lives,) Romish doctrines and practices. I would fain believe none of the language in the Prayer Book has a "popish" meaning, and that the Church of England with all her faults "does not require her members or ministers to hold the doctrine," or provides that all her ministers should profess that suc-cession as a fact, "and has not so far departed from the faith as to enjoin in any way such a monstrous fable on its members, but left it with all its consequences along with transubstantiation, mass, the real presence ; forgiveness of sins, and purgatory to a Church described centuries ago, in the spirit of prophecy by the Apostle as having " their conscience seared with a hot iron ; forbidding to marry, and commanding to abstain from meats," and whose ministers he said will " creep into houses and lead captive silly women."

www.ingramcontent.com/pod-product-compliance
Lightning Source LLC
Chambersburg PA
CBHW081453070426
42452CB00042B/2725